Producing something, as well as sharing it with the world is scary! You never understand what people will certainly consider it, as well as whether they will appreciate it. Over the past couple of years, I have actually created and also produced things, as well as have been reluctant to share primarily because of that scariness. I have actually made a decision to upgrade and add 5 new devotions to this source, putting it at 25 devotions. To help you with the Christmas season, if you begin on December 1st, you'll have a dedication daily through Xmas Day. Please make use of these for personal, family or team devotions. I additionally have the book Words of Praise as well as Psalms of Worship offered on Amazon and I wish you 'd think about purchasing those.

I say thanks to God for sending His Child, Jesus, to be our Hero, and also I am so grateful that the tale of redemption begins at Xmas. It means the globe to me as well as assists to keep me going!

I pray that this resource honors you this Christmastime. Please feel free to e-mail your responses to harmannymusic@yahoo.com in addition to having a look at my website, www.churchmusicmakers.com.

O Come, O Come, Emmanuel

Oh, come, oh, come, Emmanuel, And ransom money restricted Israel,
That mourns in lonesome expatriation here Till the Boy of God show up.
Express joy! Be glad! Emmanuel Shall concern you, O Israel!
Oh, come, our Knowledge from over, That ordered all points mightily;
To us the path of understanding program, and also teach us in her ways to
go.
Celebrate! Be glad! Emmanuel Shall come to you, O Israel!
Oh, come, oh, come, our Lord of might, That to your people on Sinai's
elevation
Express joy! Emmanuel Shall come to you, O Israel!
Oh, come O Rod of Jesse's stem, From ev'ry enemy supply them
That trust your mighty pow' r to save; Bring them in vict' ry through the
grave. Celebrate! Express joy! Emmanuel
Shall come to you, O Israel!
Oh, come, O Key of David, come, As well as widen our heav' nly
residence; Make safe the manner in which leads on high, As well as close
the path to torment.
Be glad! Be glad! Emmanuel Shall pertain to you, O Israel!
Oh, come, our Dayspring from over, And also cheer us by your
illustration nigh, Disperse the dismal clouds of evening,
Express joy! Be glad!
Shall come to you, O Israel!
Oh, come, Wish of nations, bind In one the hearts of all the human race;
Oh, bid our unfortunate departments cease, And also be on your own our
King of Peace. Express joy! Rejoice! Emmanuel
Shall come to you, O Israel!
Text: Latin, translated by John Mason Neale

Waiting is hard. Waiting is irritating. We dislike waiting. Especially currently
in our "have it now" world, waiting even a little of time drives us insane.
Envision yourself in the shoes of the Kid of Israel. They had been waiting
because the succumb to the guaranteed Messiah. All throughout the centuries,
there was hope that the Messiah would certainly get here, however they still
needed to wait. They needed to withstand slavery, expatriation, guideline by

other nations, and throughout that time, they still waited. Because of that waiting, the expectation looked to the hope as well as flexibility from oppression by others.

When Jesus was birthed, it was with little pomp as well as situation. It had not been in a royal palace that Jesus, the King of the world was born, yet a barn. He was not stocked a stylish crib, yet a feeding trough for animals. He did not have silk blankets to cover with, but itchy, scratchy, uncomfortable hay.

Rarely the assumption of a Rescuer that the Kid of Israel wanted!

Jesus was not born to alleviate earthly oppression. He was born to live a best life, pass away, climb once again, as well as ascend into paradise to prepare an area for us for infinity. A location where every little thing is ideal as well as we will certainly see God one-on-one. Since Jesus has actually come as well as we understand that He will come again, this hymn provides us factor to celebrate. It is still irritating and also tough for us to wait. We see points that sadden us. We experience pain. We have hope since we recognize that God maintains His assurances in His time, and when His timing is right, He will certainly return once again as well as take us to be with Him.

Petition: Beloved God, thank You for coming to rescue Your people from transgression and fatality. As we await Your return once again, offer us toughness and patience as we maintain our focus on You as we wait. Amen.

Savior of the Nations, Come

1. Hero of the nations, come virgin's Kid, make right here thy house!
Marvel now, O heav 'n and also planet, that the Lord chose such a birth.
2. Not of flesh as well as blood the Boy, children of the Holy One;
born of Mary ever before honored, God in flesh appears.
3. Astounding birth! O wondrous youngster of the Virgin undefiled!
By all the world disowned, still to be in heav 'n enthroned.
4. From the Daddy forth He came and returneth to the very same,
captive leading fatality as well as hell, high the song of accomplishment
swell!
5. Thou the Daddy's only Child hast o'er transgression the vict' ry won.
Limitless shall thy kingdom be; when shall we its splendors see?
6. Appreciation to God the Daddy, sing Appreciation to God the Child,
our King.
Appreciation to God the Spirit be ever before and also permanently.
Text: St. Ambrose; Translator: William M. Reynolds; Translator
(German): Martin Luther (1523)

Savior of the countries? Which nations? All of them from the moment of
Adam on. Not simply to the moment of Jesus, however all countries for all
time. Also those who
don't know or think in Jesus. Isn't that impressive? As the initial states,
"Marvel now, O paradise and planet". We are in awe as well as surprised
regarding why God, the Almighty, the all effective designer of the world
would certainly select to save His renegade, rebellious development by doing
this.
Jesus handles our human kind, but does it in the most remarkable method
possible. He is birthed of a virgin. Despite having all of our technical and
clinical expertise, we can not replicate this. As well as we never will because
it was all because of God's hand, as well as even more fantastic, His prepare
for saving the world. The story doesn't simply stop with Jesus being born.
Infants are cute as well as remarkable, however there was something a lot
more unique and incredible about Jesus.
Jesus was birthed with a single purpose. When it comes to all other children

birthed, moms and dads wonder what they will certainly become, exactly how they will certainly mature, what they will certainly perform in life. When He expanded up, Mary and also Joseph were told prior to Jesus was born what He would do. He would save all nations via His fatality on a cross as well as rebirth from the grave. Because of that job, Xmas has far more definition as well as effect in our world. It isn't nearly Jesus' birth. It had to do with the start of God's plan of redemption, planned prior to the production of the universe, put into plan at simply the correct time.

And so, as a result of the job of Jesus, all countries praise God, Papa, Child and Holy Spirit for this work of salvation, this cost-free gift that we did nothing to make other than be the receivers of God's love. It is absolutely a wonder and also we applaud God when we think and stop of that!

Prayer: Dear Jesus, thanks for concerning conserve all nations. Assist us to celebrate as well as applaud You for the spectacular work of salvation that You have actually won for us. Amen.

Hark the Glad Sound

1. Hark the delighted audio! The Rescuer comes, the Hero promised long!
Allow ev'ry heart prepare a throne, and also ev'ry voice a track.
2. He comes the pris' ners to launch in Satan's bondage held;
evictions of brass before Him burst, the iron fetters produce.
3. He comes the broken heart to bind the blood loss spirit to cure,
and also with the prizes of His elegance t' improve the humbled poor.
4. Our glad Hosannas, Royal prince of Tranquility Thy welcome shall announce;
and heav 'n' s eternal arcs ring with Thy precious Name.
Text: Philip Doddridge (1735)

Hark! It is a word from Old English that suggests "listen". Why utilize that word today? Occasionally when words are used frequently, they end up being normal and we obtain utilized to hearing them. When words aren't utilized as regularly, they can capture us unsuspecting. As well as when Jesus came as an infant, there is a lot of the story that catches people off guard. Whatever concerning Jesus was uncommon. His birth, His life, His death and His rebirth. All not normal for life in Israel during that time. Yet more, the important things sung about in this hymn share the things that the birth, life, fatality and also rebirth of Jesus brings for all mankind.

Jesus involves release the detainees. Not just those in physical jails, yet the prison that transgression brings right into our life. As Paul says, things that we do not wish to do we find ourselves doing. That is the power that sin holds over us.

Due to the fact that of Jesus, we are launched from that transgression. Jesus comes to recover the damaged heart as well as the blood loss heart.

We might still locate ourselves struggling with those hurts as well as heartaches, but depending on Jesus and also His power gives us the recovery as well as hope that we need.

Because of the job of Jesus, we can praise His name and shout "Hosanna", a foreshadowing of Palm Sunday and Jesus' triumphant entry right into Jerusalem, yet also greater than Palm Sunday, the "Hosanna" that will certainly be shouted in heaven because of His fatality, life as well as rebirth will resound! We can listen to that glad sound this Xmas period, the good news of the birth of Jesus, as well as make our hearts and lives ready for Him.

Prayer: Hark! We enjoy Your coming, Lord Jesus, and applaud You for the redemption and also recovery You have actually offered the globe. Amen.

Once He Came in Blessing

1. When He can be found in blessing, All our sickness restoring;
Came in similarity lowly, Kid of God most holy; Bore the cross to save us,
Hope and also freedom provided us.
2. Still He comes within us, Still His voice would win us From the
transgressions that harm us; Would to Fact transform us From our foolish
errors
Ere He can be found in horrors.
3. Therefore, if thou hast known Him, Not ashamed to possess Him,
Shrivel count on Him boldly Nor dost love Him coldly, He will certainly
after that obtain thee, Heal thee, and forgive thee.
4. He who thus endureth Bright incentive secureth. Come, after that, O Lord
Jesus, From our wrongs launch us; Let us right here admit Thee
Till in paradise we honor Thee.
   Text: Johann Roh; Translator (English): Catherine Winkworth

This hymn doesn't actually specifically deal with Jesus' birth, but yet in
hymnals it is categorized as an Introduction hymn. Why? Well, it is talking
about Jesus concerning planet and also what He performed in His death,
rebirth and also life. It actually does fit as an Introduction hymn. The birth,
life, fatality as well as rebirth of Jesus remedies, or heals all of our sickness,
or sins. We do have hope and freedom because of His death as well as
rebirth.

Despite our wicked nature and repeated acts of rebellion, Jesus comes to
us and also forgives our sins every single time we request for forgiveness.
This all comes from a partnership with Jesus. And also a huge part because
partnership is trusting Him. Not simply for particular things, but also for
whatever. And that's where it obtains hard. We have our very own certain
things that we wish to have the ability to regulate as well as maintain tabs
on in our life, however God wants everything. So we have to give up
control, and that's very scary! When we trust in Him, we have overall
recovery as well as mercy.

The last knowledgeable of this hymn, as numerous do, points us to
paradise. Our infinite benefit. The final knowledgeable focuses us on
counting on Jesus and sharing His name and also His tale with everybody

around us till we get to paradise and also appreciation His name forever and see Him one-on-one. Jesus pertains to earth in true blessing as a baby to live the life we could not live, die the death we win the success and also are worthy of over fatality as well as the evil one to offer us His true blessing! He is available in true blessing to give us timeless blessing!

Prayer: Dear Jesus, we thank You true blessing us with Your blessing. Help us to share that true blessing with others in our activities and words. Amen.

Lo! He Comes with Clouds Descending

1 Lo! he comes with clouds
descending, as soon as for favored
sinners slaughtered;
thousand, thousand saints attending
swell the victory of his train.
Alleluia! Alleluia!
God appears in the world to reign.
2 Ev' ry eye will currently see him,
robed in dreadful greatness;
those who evaluate naught and
offered him, pierced, and toenailed
him to the tree, deeply sobbing,
deeply sobbing,
will truth Messiah see.
3 Ev' ry sea, mountain, and island,
heav 'n and also earth, shall take off
away;
all that despise him must,
dumbfounded, listen to the trump
proclaim the day:
Concern judgment! Come to
judgment! Concern judgment, leave!
4 Now Redemption, long
anticipated, see in solemn pomp
show up!
All his saints, by guy declined, now
shall fulfill him airborne. Alleluia!
Alleluia!
See the day of God appear!
5 Yea, amen! let all love thee, high
on thine eternal throne; Hero, take
the pow'r and also glory, assert the
kingdom for thine very own. O come
quickly, O come swiftly; alleluia!

come, Lord, come.
Text: Charles Wesley (1758)

When Jesus rose into heaven, He was hidden by the clouds. And so in this hymn, we sing regarding Jesus coming from the heavens with clouds. This hymn is concerning his second coming, yet it additionally offers as a Development hymn.

Much of the themes in Introduction concentrate us not only on Jesus' very first coming, but additionally on His 2nd coming. Just as Advent reminds us to prepare for the birth of Jesus, we get on the other side of the rebirth, so we understand the full tale. We understand that Jesus will certainly come again. So, Arrival is a time of preparation throughout. Not simply for Xmas as well as the birth of Jesus, but also for His return. We do not know when it will certainly occur, so we have to constantly prepare either for His return in splendor, or for Him to call us residence to be with Him.

The final verse finishes with a phone call for Jesus to return rapidly. For us, as we wait for His second coming, we pray for Jesus to return promptly, but might we constantly be prepared at any kind of time for it to take place.

Prayer: Lord Jesus, we pray for You to find promptly. Help us await Your return. Amen.

Come, Thou Long-Expected Jesus

1. Come, thou long expected Jesus, birthed to establish thy individuals cost-free;
from our anxieties as well as transgressions launch us, allow us discover our rest in thee.
Israel's strength and consolation, hope of all the planet thou art; dear wish of every country,
delight of every hoping heart.
2. Born thy individuals to deliver, birthed a kid as well as yet a King, born to rule in us for life,
currently thy gracious kingdom bring.
By thine very own timeless spirit policy in all our hearts alone; by thine all sufficient advantage,
increase us to thy marvelous throne.
   Text: Charles Wesley

When it was the appropriate time in God's strategy, Jesus was birthed. Jesus was born to establish the people totally free from their wrongs. He was the rescuer of Israel, but even much more than that, Jesus was the hero of the entire world!

In the second verse, we see what Jesus was birthed for. He was born to provide His individuals.

power in us permanently. That is some high praise for a baby! He was the one that God guaranteed, as well as He is the fulfillment of that promise. The birth of Jesus offers the whole world due to God maintaining that promise in His most ideal way feasible. Jesus comes to earth, humble and also lowly, born in a barn, laid in a manger, yet due to His fatality, resurrection and also life, God positions Him on the throne over all points. Yet more than that, Jesus does not just remain on His throne and look down on us, He calls us and brings us as much as His throne. Knowing that, it still makes it hard to be client and wait, however it does make it a little easier. So we wait for His 2nd coming with hope and expectancy.

Petition: Beloved Jesus, You came as an infant, and also we await

Your 2nd can be found in splendor. Aid us to patiently wait on Your arrival. Amen.

Joy to the Globe

Delight to the globe! The Lord has actually come Allow planet obtain her King!

Allow every heart prepare His room And heaven as well as nature sing

And also paradise and nature sing

And paradise, and heaven and also nature sing

Joy to the World

Plains, hillsides and rocks Repeat the seeming joy Repeat the sounding
joy Repeat, repeat the audio happiness
No more let wrong and sorrow grow Neither thorns infest the ground
He pertains to make His true blessings circulation
Much as the curse is discovered Far as the curse is found
Far as, far as menstruation is discovered
He rules the globe with reality and elegance And also makes the countries
confirm
The splendors of His nonpartisanship And also wonders of His love
And also marvels of is love
As well as marvels and also wonders of His love
Text: Isaac Watts

One of the most precious Xmas hymns was not meant to be a hymn
concerning Jesus's initial coming, however concerning His second coming.
Knowledgeable 4 of the Psalm is where that opening up expression comes
from. with songs".

Whether we use this hymn for Christmas or any type of other time in the
year, it is essential to bear in mind that our feedback to what God has
actually performed in our lives should be pleasure. All frequently, we're
bordered by God's blessing as well as it comes to be ordinary. We lose that
feeling of awe and happiness in our lives. And also when we checked out
Bible like Psalm 98, or various other verses that advise us of God's power
and greatness, we go back to that joy as well as wonder as well as God and
also what He does in our lives.

The final verse of this hymn reminds not just of God's nonpartisanship, but His love as well as elegance that comes to us each and also every day. God's grace and love come to us daily, and when we are in tune with it, we have that happiness. As well as when that delight is transmittable from us to others around us, people will discover and also wonder why we are different.

Petition: Precious God, thanks for giving me the happiness that originates from seeing Your elegance, mercy as well as love in action. Aid me to share that pleasure with others. Amen.

O Little Town of Bethlehem

O little town of Bethlehem, how still we see thee lie!
Above thy dreamless and deep sleep, the quiet celebrities
go by. Yet in thy dark roads shineth the everlasting
Light.
The hopes and also fears of all the years are met in thee
this evening.
For Christ is birthed of Mary, and gathered all above,
While people sleep, the angels keep their watch of
wondering love. O morning stars, with each other
declare the divine birth
And also applauds sing to God, the King, and tranquility
to guys in the world.
How quietly, just how calmly, the remarkable Present is
giv' n!
So God conveys to human hearts the blessings of His
heaven. No ear may hear His coming, however in this
world of sin,
Where meek souls will obtain Him still, the dear Christ
goes into in.
O holy Youngster of Bethlehem, descend to us, we pray;
Exiled our wrongs as well as enter in, be birthed to us
today.
We hear the Christmas angels the terrific glad tidings
tell: Oh, concerned us, follow with us, our Lord
Emmanuel!
Text: Philip Brooks

This hymn casts an idyllic photo that we assume of at Xmas. What
we do know is that the quantity of individuals in the city swelled due to
the fact that of the census so a lot that there was no space for Mary and
also Joseph. Whatever the level of sound, many in the city of
Bethlehem did not know how much the world had actually changed that
evening because of the birth of a child.

In spectacular fashion, God created the world. In stunning fashion, throughout the Old Testimony, God provided and rescued His individuals.

Whether that was parting the Red Sea, tearing down the wall surfaces of Jericho, or any type of other remarkable tale, God showed up as well as showed His power in incredible fashion. When the time to rescue the globe comes, there is no large

Why does God work in this method? It can really well be that He functions in this means to show the humbleness and perfection of Jesus, taking on human form to conserve the globe.

We enjoy the resulting the child, as well as yet, when we take a look around in this globe today, we see several who are asleep to the Word of God as well as asleep to the expertise of Jesus. Similar to the shepherds told and went every person about the birth of baby Jesus, it is entrusted on us to share the good news about God, His love and mercy shown via the birth of the Savior in a manger in Bethlehem.

Petition: Precious God, thanks for revealing Your love to us by sending out Jesus to be birthed as an infant in Bethlehem. Aid us to share the news about You to every person we enter into call with. Amen.

O Holy Night

O Holy Evening! The stars are vibrantly beaming, It is the night of the dear Saviour's birth.
Lengthy lay the world in wrong as well as error pining. Till He showed up as well as the Spirit felt its well worth. A thrill of hope the weary world rejoices, For yonder breaks a glorious and new morn.
Loss on your knees! Oh, hear the angel voices! O night divine, the evening when Christ was birthed; O night, O Holy Night, O night divine!
O evening, O Holy Evening, O evening divine!
Led by the light of faith serenely beaming, With radiant hearts by His cradle we stand. O'er the globe a star is swiftly dazzling,
Currently come the wisemen from out of the Orient land. The King of kings lay therefore lowly manger;
In all our trials birthed to be our pals.
He understands our need, our weakness is no unfamiliar person, Witness your King! Prior to him lowly bend!
Witness your King! Before him lowly flex!
Really He showed us to love each other, His legislation is love and His gospel is tranquility.
Chains he will damage, for the slave is our brother. As well as in his name all injustice shall stop.
Pleasant hymns of delight in happy carolers raising we, With all our hearts we commend His holy name.
Christ is the Lord! After that ever before, ever before praise we, His power as well as glory ever before extra announce!
His power and glory ever a lot more proclaim!
Text: Adolphe Charles Adams

On the initial Christmas evening, also though the globe was uninformed, it received its Rescuer. God sent His Child, Jesus, to take on our human form, and also
live that best life that we can not reside on our very own.
It is impressive to quit and also ponder that no matter what our challenges or battles in life, Jesus understands those difficulties or struggles. Since Jesus is God, He took our human type and conserved us

by living completely. Whenever we struggle with difficulties in life, we can lean on Jesus as well as His understanding of our experiences.

The last verse focuses on our takeaway in our world. When Jesus was asked what the greatest commandment in Bible was, his reply was "Love the Lord with every one of your heart, soul mind as well as stamina as well as like your next-door neighbor as yourself." We have a hard time to do both of these, but Jesus offered us that utmost example in His fatality, resurrection as well as life. The world today needs to see love modeled and also shown more and more. Jesus claimed, "Greater love has nobody than this: to put down one's life for one's buddies." Which was the instance provided to us in the life of Jesus, which started at Xmas. Which is the factor we commemorate!

Prayer: Dear God, thanks for that Holy evening that You provided Jesus to the world. Thanks for His perfect life, saving us from our wrongs. Amen.

Angels We Have Heard on High!

Angels we have actually listened to over Sweetly vocal singing o'er the levels, As well as the hills in reply Echoing their wondrous strains.
Gloria, in excelsis Deo Gloria, in excelsis Deo!
Shepherds, why this jubilee?
Why your wonderful strains lengthen? What the gladsome tidings be Which inspire your beautiful tune?
Gloria, in excelsis Deo!
Gloria, in excelsis Deo!
Concern Bethlehem and see.
Christ Whose birth the angels sing; Come, love on bended knee, Christ the Lord, the newborn King.
Gloria, in excelsis Deo!
Gloria, in excelsis Deo!
See Him in a manger laid, Whom the choirs of angels praise; Mary, Joseph, provide your help, While our hearts crazy we increase.
Gloria, in excelsis Deo!
Gloria, in excelsis Deo!
Text: French Carol

Throughout the tale of the Nativity, angels play a primary duty. From the angel showing up to Mary, the angel showing up to Zechariah and Elizabeth,

and also the angels showing up to the guards, God carriers, the angels, are sharing fortunately. This hymn focuses extra on the angels showing up to the shepherds. Can you picture what it would certainly resemble to hear the audio of every one of the angels vocal singing appreciation to God? What would certainly that appear resemble?

It was more than likely a peaceful night. That quiet was damaged by the noise of one angel, after that countless more declaring the news that the Savior of the globe has been birthed. They hurried off to see the child as well as prayer Him.

We are phoned call to join the guards in applauding God for the present of His Boy, Jesus. We see the child Jesus born in the manger, as well as we celebrate and also rejoice. We understand the rest of the tale, that Jesus died, climbed and has actually risen to paradise to prepare an area for us, and also it makes our rejoicing and commemorating at Christmas that much greater. We sing our "Gloria in excelsis Deo" with our entire heart and also voice due to the fact that we celebrate God's outstanding operate in our lives!

Prayer: Lord God, we thank You for sending Your Kid, Jesus, to be our Rescuer. Thank You for letting us understand the entire tale of redemption, as well as allow us prayer You this Christmas with our entire heart as well as voice. Amen.

Mary, Did You Know

Mary did you understand that your child will some day stroll on water?
Mary did you recognize that your baby kid will save our boys as well as
children? Did you recognize that your child has come to make you brand-
new?
This child that you've provided, will quickly provide you.
Mary did you recognize that your child will give sight to a blind man?
Mary did you understand that your infant boy will soothe a tornado with
his hand? Did you recognize that your infant child has walked where
angels walked?
As well as when your kiss your little baby, you have actually kissed the
face of God. Oh Mary did you know
The blind will see, the deaf will certainly hear, the dead will live once
more. The lame will jump, the dumb will certainly speak, the praises of
the lamb
Mary did you know that your baby child is Lord of all production?
Mary did you understand that your infant child would certainly eventually
rule the nations? Did you know that your child boy is paradise's perfect
Lamb?
This sleeping child you're holding is the wonderful I am
Text: Mark Lowry

Very commonly in life we make decisions, choices or have things occur
that we do not understand the end result. When those things take place,
how we respond as well as react is important.

As well as then God disrupts. The angel tells Mary that she will
certainly give birth to a child. Not just any kind of child, however she will
certainly lug the Boy of God.

Did Mary know what Jesus would certainly come to be? The Bible
offers us marginal details. We know that she was informed that Jesus is the
Child of God, yet that's virtually concerning it. Would certainly she have
responded differently if she knew what points Jesus would certainly
undergo? Would certainly she have responded in a different way if she
recognized what He would certainly do? We know that Mary was close to
Jesus throughout His life. Being an excellent mom, she was there for the

initial steps, along with the last steps to the cross.

Whether Mary knew what Jesus would certainly be when He matured, or what Jesus would do, we do not know. We know that God utilized her to be the mother of our Hero as well as functioned via her to provide us a response of tranquility as well as count on in God and His plan as well as objective for life.

Petition: Beloved God, we thank You for being with us and providing us Your Boy, Jesus. Thanks for the reaction of Mary, as well as we ask that You provide us peace as well as count on Your strategy. Amen.

Silent Night

Silent night, Holy night
All is tranquil, all is intense
Round yon virgin, mom and also youngster
Holy infant, tender and also mild
Sleep in beautiful peace,
Sleep in divine tranquility.
Silent evening,
Divine night Son of God, love's pure light
Radiant beams from thy holy face
With the dawn of redeeming elegance,
Jesus, Lord at thy birth
Jesus, Lord at thy birth.
Quiet night,
Divine night Shepherds quake, at the sight
Magnificences stream from paradise above
Heavenly, hosts sing Hallelujah.
Christ the Hero is born,
Christ the Rescuer is born.
Text: Franz Gruber

If you have actually ever before been around and also experienced giving birth, you recognize that there is nothing calm concerning it! To add to it, the city of Bethlehem had plenty of extra individuals and also pets in it due to the census, and also it more than most likely was not a tranquil and silent night. None of us were there, so we do not understand whether or not that evening was tranquil and quiet.

For the shepherds, it was an evening like most others. They were out in the fields, yet after that, an angel appeared. That is not something that they were accustomed to seeing. Of training course, the angel had to inform them "Do not be scared", as fear would certainly be the most ideal reaction for most! And then, the silence of the night is broken even extra. There is a heavenly carolers of

angels, as well as they begin vocal singing! Not a quiet point! This was a night for expressing joy!

In our lives during the prep work to and also the event of Christmas, it appears that a lot of our nights are far from silent. From Xmas parties, to school functions as well as much, far more, there is lots that is taking place in our lives. But we need to remember the reason as well as stop why we commemorate Christmas. God liked the globe so much that He sent out Jesus as a child, birthed in Bethlehem, to die on the cross as well as save us from our transgressions. We can be and celebrate in admiration of just how much God loves us when we focus on God and also His gift of salvation to us at Christmastime!

Prayer: Dear God, thanks for Your present of Jesus, the child born in the manger, to be our Hero. Assist us to be focused on You as well as the genuine reason that we commemorate at Xmas. Amen.

The First Noel

The First Noel, the Angels did claim
Was to specific bad shepherds in areas as they lay In fields where they lay
keeping their lamb
On a cold winter season's evening that was so deep. Noel, Noel, Noel,
Noel
Birthed is the King of Israel!
They looked up and also saw a star Shining in the East past them far As
well as to the planet it gave wonderful light
And so it proceeded both day and night. Noel, Noel, Noel, Noel
Birthed is the King of Israel!
And by the light of that very same star 3 Wise males came from country
much To seek for a King was their intent
As well as to adhere to the celebrity any place it went. Noel, Noel, Noel,
Noel
Born is the King of Israel!
This star attracted nigh to the northwest O'er Bethlehem it took its rest
And there it did both Time out and remain Right o'er the place where
Jesus lay. Noel, Noel, Noel, Noel
Birthed is the King of Israel!
After that entered in those Wise guys 3 Full reverently upon their knee
And supplied there in His existence Their gold and myrrh as well as
incense. Noel, Noel, Noel, Noel
Born is the King of Israel!
Let us all with one accord Sing commends to our divine Lord
That hath made Heaven and planet of nought As well as with his blood
mankind has actually purchased.
Noel, Noel, Noel, Noel Born is the King of Israel!

Text: English

The shepherds were out in their areas and they saw an angel who
informed them that the Savior of the globe had been born. They saw the
infant Jesus, worshiped Him, and also after that went as well as told
others.

The wise men bring a little even more of an interesting story. Matthew 2 once again, refers to the "home" where Jesus was. Based on Herod's feedback of killing child kids 2 years old as well as under, as Jesus would certainly have probably been around 2 at this point.

We participate in the songs and also praise of the guards and the wise guys of vocal singing "Noel! Born is the King of Israel". It was as a result of His birth, life, fatality and also rebirth that we have redemption. Yet it needed to begin with His birth. Therefore we celebrate!

Petition: Precious God, thank You for offering the shepherds and also wise males a chance to witness Jesus with their own eyes. Thank You for offering us eyes of confidence to see You and count on what You have provided for us. Amen.

What Child is This?

What kid is this, who, put to
rest, On Mary's lap is sleeping,
Whom angels greet with anthems
pleasant While shepherds see are
maintaining?
This, this is Christ the King,
Whom shepherds guard and angels
sing; Haste, rush to bring Him admire,
The infant, the child of Mary!
Why lies He in such mean estate
Where ox and also ass are feeding?
Good Christian, worry: for
sinners right here The quiet
Word is begging.
Nails, spear will puncture him
with, The Cross be borne for
me, for you; Hail, hail words
Made Flesh,
The babe, the son of Mary!
Bring Him incense, gold, and
also incense; Come, peasant,
king, to have Him!
The King of Kings redemption
brings; Allow caring hearts
enthrone Him!
Raise, increase the song above!
The virgin sings her lullaby.
Pleasure! joy! for Christ is
birthed, The infant, the kid of
Mary!
Text: William Chatterton Dix

This hymn is just one of the most beloved songs of youngsters. When we
see infants, especially resting children, they are so tranquil and also it

provides us tranquility. Jesus was not laid in a comfy, expensive baby crib with soft as well as cozy coverings, however a feeding trough for animals, lined with hay. You understand exactly how soft and also comfy the hay is not if you have actually ever been to a ranch or on a hay flight! It is scratchy, awkward and also scratchy. When we lay infants down now, we want the softest and most comfortable bed linen we can find. Mary as well as Joseph made use of

what was nearby as well as accessible.

The 3rd knowledgeable of this hymn is a prayer for Jesus to stay near to us regardless of where we go. As well as we understand by checking out Scripture that God is with us. It is promised in the Bible, and also we know that God does not neglect His pledges. The 3rd knowledgeable is a prayer for God's true blessing on children as well as asking God to take us all, no matter what our age, to heaven. It also full of words of convenience and hope, knowing that whatever we experience in life, Jesus will be by our side forever. He will, at the end of our days here in the world, call us to paradise to live eternally with Him.

And also it is a pointer for all of us to have faith like a kid. As well as for that, we applaud and also say thanks to God for the present of Jesus as well as the present of faith.

Petition: Dear God, we thanks for Jesus, the baby birthed in Bethlehem, as well as we thank You for the faith that You have put in our hearts. Remind us that You are with us and caring for us. Amen.

Away in a Manger

Mild Mary laid her Child lowly in a manger;
There He lay, the undefiled, to the globe a
Stranger: Such an Infant in such a place, can
He be the Hero?
Ask the saved of all the race who have actually
located His favor.
Angels sang regarding His birth;
sensible males sought and found
Him; Heaven's star beamed
vibrantly forth, magnificence
around Him: Shepherds saw the
fascinating sight, listened to the
angels singing; All the levels were
lit that evening, all capitals were
calling.
Gentle Mary laid her Youngster lowly in a manger; He is still the
undefiled, yet no more a stranger: Child of God, of modest birth,
lovely the story;
Praise His Name in all the planet,
hail the King of magnificence!
   Text: Charles Gabriel

The story of God sending out Jesus appears a little odd and out of area, does
not it? Jesus being born as a baby? If He's God, why not simply appear on the
planet?
God humbling Himself to handle our human type and also rescue us. This
humbling came consequently of our transgression, and also most
significantly, because of God's great love for us.
This hymn inquires about this baby birthed in a manger, "can He be the
Rescuer?" When children our born, moms and dads and also member of the
family visualize and also imagine what the child will do as well as who the
youngster will come to be. Even though Mary and Joseph were told that Jesus
would certainly be the rescuer of the globe, it does not fit our expectation, or
the expectations of the people at the time. God does that so frequently in our

lives. He does not fit into the ways or concepts that we anticipate Him to, however He acts in His perfect timing. And also because of that, we wind up being surprised and awed.

In the last knowledgeable, Jesus is no more the baby in the manger, yet the climbed and also worshiped Rescuer. He disappears an unfamiliar person to the world; He is the redeemer of the globe. The tale of God humbling Himself is not one that Hollywood can ever before create, but it is the most best tale ever before created, because of the author. The story that God composes is completely done, shows His mercy and love that is completely unjust. And for that, we are grateful.

Prayer: Precious God, we thanks for Your grace and also grace shown to us by humbling Yourself to being born as an infant as well as being our Rescuer. Thank You for creating an incredible, perfect as well as beautiful tale. Amen.

Gentle Mary Laid Her Child

Gentle Mary laid her Child lowly in a manger;
There He lay, the undefiled, to the world a
Stranger: Such a Babe in such a place, can He be
the Savior?
Ask the saved of all the race who have found His favor.

Angels sang about His birth; wise men sought and found
Him; Heaven's star shone brightly forth, glory all around
Him: Shepherds saw the wondrous sight, heard the angels
singing; All the plains were lit that night, all the hills were
ringing.

Gentle Mary laid her Child lowly in a manger;
He is still the undefiled, but no more a
stranger: Son of God, of humble birth,
beautiful the story;
Praise His Name in all the earth, hail the King of glory!
Text: Joseph Cook

The story of God sending Jesus seems a little odd and out of place,
doesn't it? It doesn't fit the script of the Savior of the world coming to
heroically save the world. At least not how Hollywood would write it.
There is so much that doesn't fit. Jesus being born as a baby? If He's God,
why not just appear on the earth? Born in a manger, not a palace? Angels
appearing to shepherds? The whole story is about humility, not majesty or
pomp and circumstance.
God humbling Himself to take on our human form and rescue us. This
humbling came as a consequence of our sin, and most importantly, because
of God's great love for us.

This hymn asks about this baby born in a manger, "can He be the
Savior?" When babies our born, parents and family members imagine and
dream of what the child will do and who the child will become. Even
though Mary and Joseph were told that Jesus would be the savior of the

world, it does not fit our expectation, or the expectations of the people at the time. But God does that so often in our lives. He does not fit into the ways or ideas that we expect Him to, but He acts in His perfect timing. And because of that, we end up being amazed and awed.

In the final verse, Jesus is no longer the baby in the manger, but the risen and exalted Savior. He is no more a stranger to the world; He is the redeemer of the world. The story of God humbling Himself is not one that Hollywood could ever write, but it is the most perfect story ever created, because of the author. The story that God writes is perfectly done, shows His mercy and love that is completely undeserved. And for that, we are thankful.

Prayer: Dear God, we thank You for Your grace and mercy shown to us by humbling Yourself to being born as a baby and being our Savior. Thank You for writing an amazing, beautiful and perfect story. Amen.

God Rest Ye Merry, Gentlemen

God rest ye merry, gentlemen, let nothing you dismay, Remember
Christ our Savior was born on Christmas Day;
To save us all from Satan's power when we were gone astray. O
tidings of comfort and joy, comfort and joy;
O tidings of comfort and joy.

In Bethlehem, in Israel, this blessèd Babe was born,
And laid within a manger upon this blessèd morn;
The which His mother Mary did nothing take in scorn. O
tidings of comfort and joy, comfort and joy;
O tidings of comfort and joy.

From God our heavenly Father a blessèd angel came; And
unto certain shepherds brought tidings of the same;
How that in Bethlehem was born the Son of God by name. O
tidings of comfort and joy, comfort and joy;
O tidings of comfort and joy.

"Fear not, then," said the angel, "Let nothing you afright
This day is born a Savior of a pure Virgin bright,
To free all those who trust in Him from Satan's power and might." O
tidings of comfort and joy, comfort and joy;
O tidings of comfort and joy.

The shepherds at those tidings rejoiced much in mind, And left
their flocks a-feeding in tempest, storm and wind,
And went to Bethl'em straightaway this blessèd Babe to find. O
tidings of comfort and joy, comfort and joy;
O tidings of comfort and joy.

But when to Bethlehem they came where our dear Savior lay,
They found Him in a manger where oxen feed on hay;
His mother Mary kneeling unto the Lord did pray. O
tidings of comfort and joy, comfort and joy;

O tidings of comfort and joy.

Now to the Lord sing praises all you within this place,
And with true love and brotherhood each other now
embrace; This holy tide of Christmas all others doth deface.
O tidings of comfort and joy, comfort and
joy; O tidings of comfort and joy.

God bless the ruler of this house, and send him long to
reign, And many a merry Christmas may live to see again;
Among your friends and kindred that live both far and
near— That God send you a happy new year, happy new
year,
And God send you a happy new year.
Text: Traditional English

The first line of this hymn is a bit confusing. God rest ye? And merry
gentlemen? What does this mean? Well, this hymn first appeared in the mid
1700s, so there was probably different meaning to those words. In spite of
the confusion of the first line, this hymn is a great reminder of the Christmas
story. Knowing that the whole reason that Jesus came as a baby was to
defeat the devil and his power gives us plenty of reason for comfort and joy.

The seventh verse of this hymn gives us the results of God's redeeming
work. We gather together and sing praises to God. We love and care for
each other, looking out for the needs of one another. But sometimes, it
seems like it only happens around Christmas time. We seem to forget the
comfort and joy that comes at Christmas throughout the year. Sometimes at
Christmas, we still lose sight of the comfort and joy.

The final verse gives us that reminder of the Christmas spirit. Asking for
God's blessing, not only for us, but for others. It seems that sometimes we
think about others at Christmas time, and when Christmas is past, we go
back to thinking about ourselves. We forget about the comfort and joy that
comes from the story of salvation. But we have the opportunity to come
back to the reminder of the story of salvation and are reminded of the

comfort and joy that comes from it.

Prayer: Thank You God for giving us the comfort and joy that comes from Your salvation. Help us to be thinking of others not only at Christmas, but all throughout the year. Amen.

We Three Kings

We three kings of Orient are
Bearing gifts we traverse afar
Field and fountain, moor and mountain
Following yonder star
O Star of wonder, star of night Star
with royal beauty bright Westward
leading, still proceeding Guide us to
thy Perfect Light

Born a King on Bethlehem's plain
Gold I bring to crown Him again
King forever, ceasing never
Over us all to reign
O Star of wonder, star of night Star
with royal beauty bright Westward
leading, still proceeding Guide us to
Thy perfect light

Frankincense to offer have I
Incense owns a Deity nigh
Prayer and praising, all men raising
Worship Him, God most high
O Star of wonder, star of night Star
with royal beauty bright Westward
leading, still proceeding Guide us to
Thy perfect light

Myrrh is mine, its bitter perfume
Breathes of life of gathering gloom
Sorrowing, sighing, bleeding, dying
Sealed in the stone-cold tomb
O Star of wonder, star of night Star
with royal beauty bright Westward
leading, still proceeding Guide us to

Thy perfect light

Glorious now behold Him
arise King and God and
Sacrifice Alleluia, Alleluia
Earth to heav'n replies
O Star of wonder, star of night
Star with royal beauty bright
Westward leading, still
proceeding Guide us to Thy
perfect light
Text: John H. Hopkins

The three kings. It could have been more, but because there are three gifts, it is assumed that there were three kings. Whether there were three or more, their part in the Christmas story is very important. It shows God's power and majesty reaching beyond the children of Israel. These kings more than likely knew about the promises of the Messiah, and saw the star. They followed the star for probably about two years. When they found Jesus, they gave Him their gifts.

The gift of gold shows Jesus' majesty and kingship. For those who know the whole story, we know that Jesus is the king of the universe and is God. Yet, He humbled Himself and took on our flesh and lived the perfect life that we cannot live on our own.

The gift of frankincense is a reminder of worship. Incense is used in worship, and we worship God for sending Jesus to be our Savior. It is a fragrant smell, one used to cover up unseemly smells. Jesus was the incense over our sins, but He did far more than just covering up the stench of them. He removed them completely. We remember and ponder what God has done and continues to do in our lives and we give Him all glory and honor.

The gift of myrrh foretells what is to come for Jesus. His bitter suffering and death is the reason that He came to earth. But, believers know the rest of the story. Jesus died, yes, but he rose from the dead and ascended into heaven. But without the sorrow and bitterness, there is no joy. And if there is no birth, there is no life, death and resurrection. So we celebrate God's revealing of Himself to us through Jesus.

Prayer: Dear God, thank You for leading the kings to worship Jesus. Be with us as we follow Your Word to the manger this year and every year. Amen.

It Came Upon the Midnight Clear

It came upon the midnight clear,
That glorious song of old,
From angels bending near the earth, To
touch their harps of gold:
"Peace on the earth, goodwill to men
From heavens all gracious King!" The
world in solemn stillness lay
To hear the angels sing.

Still through the cloven skies they come,
With peaceful wings unfurled;
And still their heavenly music floats
O'er all the weary world:
Above its sad and lowly plains
They bend on hovering wing, And
ever o'er its Babel sounds The
blessed angels sing.

O ye beneath life's crushing load,
Whose forms are bending low, Who
toil along the climbing way With
painful steps and slow;
Look now, for glad and golden hours
Come swiftly on the wing;
Oh rest beside the weary road
And hear the angels sing.

For lo! the days are hastening on, By
prophets seen of old,
When with the ever-circling years
Shall come the time foretold,
When the new heaven and earth shall own
The Prince of Peace, their King,
And the whole world send back the song

Which now the angels sing.
Text: Edmund H. Sears

When you look at many Christmas carols, you notice a lot of focus on angels. And it is with good reason. When angels appear, there is something major happening. When the angel appears to the shepherds, the first words the angel said was, "do not be afraid." It is not an everyday occurrence to see angels. But because of the angels heralding the good news of the birth of Jesus, the shepherds go to the manger, see Jesus with their own eyes, and worship Him.

The third verse gives hope for those who are struggling. When we focus on the song of the angels, there is rest and there is hope. The struggles in this life do weigh us down from time to time. We have plenty of ups and downs, be it with health, finances, relationships and more. And when those things start to weigh us down, we can stop and listen to the sound of the angels singing and be reminded of God's love and mercy.

The final verse reminds us that not only has Jesus come to earth, lived a perfect life in our place, died, rose and went to heaven, but He is also coming back again to take us to be with Him. It was a long wait for the believers until Jesus came, and it continues to be a wait for us. Until we get to heaven, we are reminded of the angels' song, and we know that one day, when we get to heaven, we will join with those angels in singing praise to God.

Prayer: Thank You, God, for the gift of the song of angels that gives us peace and hope. Help us to remember the song of the angels in our times of struggle as we await the day that You call us home and we can join in singing Your praises. Amen.

Oh Come, All Ye Faithful

Oh, come, all ye
faithful, Joyful and
triumphant!
Oh, come ye, oh, come ye to
Bethlehem; Come and behold him
Born the king of angels:
Oh, come, let us adore
him, Oh, come, let us
adore him, Oh, come, let
us adore him, Christ the
Lord.

Highest, most holy,
Light of light
eternal, Born of a
virgin,
A mortal he
comes; Son of the
Father
Now in flesh appearing!
Oh, come, let us adore
him, Oh, come, let us
adore him, Oh, come, let
us adore him, Christ the
Lord.

Sing, choirs of
angels, Sing in
exultation,
Sing, all ye citizens of heaven
above! Glory to God
In the highest:
Oh, come, let us adore
him, Oh, come, let us

adore him, Oh, come, let
us adore him, Christ the
Lord.
Text: John Francis Wade

When we look at the story of Jesus's birth as a baby, we are compelled to
come to the manger and adore Him. Why? God loved us with a love that is
beyond our comprehension. We deserve death and hell, but because of
God's
mercy, and because of the death and resurrection of Jesus, we are
forgiven. This makes us full of joy and give God our praise and
adoration.

Jesus is the Son of God the Father, appearing in flesh here on earth. He is
the Word of God in human form. He comes with humility, not born in a
fancy and extravagant palace, but a barn. He was not born with royal blood,
but was the son of a carpenter. Nothing at all distinguished Him from
anyone else.
Outside of the angels and the star, of course!

We go to the manger and worship. We give God our praise and thanks
for what He does in our lives. We adore Him for His rescuing us from our
sin.
We join with the angels in the hymn of heaven, giving God glory, honor
and praise for His love and mercy. Without God's mercy, love and
forgiveness, we would not be able to exist or do anything at all. For that, we
give God our adoration and praise!

*Prayer: Thank You, God, for Your gift of Jesus. We give You praise
and adoration for Your salvation, started at the manger in Bethlehem.
Amen.*

Hark the Herald Angels Sing!

Hark the herald angels sing
"Glory to the newborn King!
Peace on earth and mercy mild
God and sinners reconciled"
Joyful, all ye nations rise
Join the triumph of the skies
With the angelic host proclaim:
"Christ is born in Bethlehem"
Hark! The herald angels sing
"Glory to the newborn King!"

Christ by highest heav'n adored
Christ the everlasting Lord!
Late in time behold Him come
Offspring of a Virgin's womb
Veiled in flesh the Godhead see
Hail the incarnate Deity
Pleased as man with man to dwell
Jesus, our Emmanuel
Hark! The herald angels sing
"Glory to the newborn King!"

Hail the heav'n-born Prince of Peace!
Hail the Son of Righteousness!
Light and life to all He brings
Ris'n with healing in His wings
Mild He lays His glory by Born
that man no more may die Born
to raise the sons of earth Born to
give them second birth Hark!
The herald angels sing "Glory to
the newborn King!"
Text: Charles Wesley

Imagine being a shepherd, out in the field watching your sheep. It is a quiet night, and you are finding yourself trying to fight off sleep and stay awake. When all of sudden, out of nowhere, a bright light appears shining brighter than the sun. That's no light. It's an angel! You tremble in fear. The angel speaks and says, "Do not be afraid; for behold, I bring you good tidings of great joy! A baby has been born! He is Christ the Lord! You will find Him in a manger wrapped in swaddling clothes." And then the sky is filled with angels and they start to sing! What a beautiful and amazing sound. You have to pause for a few moments to let all of this sink in. A baby? In a manger?
Christ the Lord? Why did the angel tell me this? I'm just a lowly shepherd! But the shepherds go and find Jesus. They worship Him and then tell everyone they see the good news.

The story of the birth of Jesus is not just good news. This is amazing news.
This is transforming news. Why? God promised to send a Savior starting in the garden of Eden. And God does not forget His promises. God shows His love and mercy in an unbelievable way by sending His one and only Son to live the life that we cannot live, die on the cross, taking our sins with Him, and rising again from the grave. But it starts with the birth. The shepherds were probably not anyone's first choice to be the messengers of the good news. But that's how God works. He takes the things and the people that the world thinks aren't the first choice or the best choice and He uses them.

For us, we can sing the words of that final verse "Hail the heaven-born Prince of Peace! Hail the Son of Righteousness!" with all of our hearts, knowing that God has called us to be His witnesses, telling the world about what Jesus has done. We do not have to be the most eloquent, or have all of the answers. God will do that work. But we need to be like the shepherds and see what God has done for us, and tell everyone in sight!

Prayer: Dear God, thank You for using the shepherds to spread the good news about the birth of Jesus. Use us as well to proclaim the good news wherever we go. Amen.

Welcome to Our World

Tears are falling, hearts are
breaking How we need to hear
from God
You've been promised, we've been waiting

Welcome Holy Child
Welcome Holy Child

Hope that you don't mind our
manger How I wish we would have
known But long-awaited Holy
Stranger Make Yourself at home
Please make Yourself at home
Bring Your peace into our
violence Bid our hungry souls be
filled
Word now breaking Heaven's silence

Welcome to our world
Welcome to our world

Fragile finger sent to heal us
Tender brow prepared for thorn
Tiny heart whose blood will save
us Unto us is born
Unto us is born
So wrap our injured flesh around
You Breathe our air and walk our
sod
Rob our sin and make us holy

Perfect Son of God
Perfect Son of God
Welcome to our

world *Text: Chris Rice*

Jesus, the perfect Son of God, the Word of God, came from heaven and took on human form. Stop to think about that. God Himself became a human.

The creator became the creation. Why? To redeem the creation. This fallen, broken, rebellious and self-centered creation needed a redeemer. The only one that could redeem it was the creator Himself. But if God spoke all creation into existence, why couldn't He fix it another way? He is intimately connected to humanity. Every other aspect of creation was spoken into existence. Humanity was physically touched by God. Created out of the dirt, fashioned with God's own hand, having life breathed into it by God's own breath. Made in God's image and called very good. Yet, because of one choice by God's creation, that perfect nature became flawed. There was no quick fix here. There was no other way. The creator, intimately connected and hands on with His creation, would have to be hands on and intimately connected with the redemption of the creation. But why? That's the best part. The creator loves His creation, no matter how broken and flawed, and because of that love that we cannot understand, God was willing to make the ultimate sacrifice for us, His creation.

God took His perfection and placed it in humanity. Jesus took on our skin and bones and was born in humility. The perfect Son of God, surrounded by angels in heaven, became a human being. He took the brokenness and made it perfect once again. He taught and explained the heart and mind of God. But it was not fully understood. As part of God's plan, Jesus was to be falsely accused, arrested, beaten and tortured, and killed. Who would sign on to this choice? This is God's love for His creation. He would willingly make this sacrifice to rescue and redeem His creation.

When we celebrate Christmas, we do not celebrate merely a birth. We celebrate God's love. We celebrate that restoration that could only happen because of God's intimate and personal connection to us, His creation. As John 3:16 puts it so perfectly, "For God so loved the world that he gave his one and only Son, that whoever believes in him shall not perish but have eternal life." This is what we celebrate at Christmas. For because God loved us, He gave His one and only Son, born and laid in a manger, so that we, His creation, can put our faith and trust in Him, and have eternal life. That is the beautiful story that begins with the birth of Jesus.

Prayer: Dear God, thank You for coming to our world, living a perfect life and redeeming us. We ask You to help us rejoice and be thankful for Your love and help us to tell the story to those who need to hear it. Amen.

Angels from the Realms of Glory

Angels from the realms of glory,
Wing your flight o'er all the earth;
Ye who sang creation's story,
Now proclaim Messiah's birth:
Come and worship,
Come and worship,
Worship Christ, the newborn King!

Shepherds, in the fields abiding,
Watching o'er your flocks by night,
God with man is now residing,
Yonder shines the infant Light;
Come and worship,
Come and worship,
Worship Christ, the newborn King!

Sages, leave your contemplations,
Brighter visions beam afar;
Seek the great desire of nations,
Ye have seen His natal star;
Come and worship,
Come and worship,
Worship Christ, the newborn King!

Saints before the altar bending,
Watching long in hope and fear,
Suddenly the Lord, descending,
In His temple shall appear:
Come and worship,
Come and worship,
Worship Christ, the newborn King!
Text: James Montgomery

Worship. The word is used very often in church, but what does it mean?

Some churches refer to it as their corporate gatherings. Some churches refer to it as their music time in their corporate gatherings. The word "worship" is defined in the dictionary as "the feeling or expression of reverence and adoration for a deity." Reverence and adoration. Worship is not tied to a specific location, and it can be with or without music. Worship is a feeling or expression. In the Christmas story, we hear about that worship coming from multiple sources. The angels first worshiped by telling the shepherds about the baby in the manger by singing, "Glory to God in the highest! And on earth, peace, goodwill among men." The shepherds worshiped when they followed what the angels said, found Jesus, and gave Him reverence and adoration. The wise men, or kings, followed the star for about 2 years until they were led to Jesus. Their worship was offering gifts of gold, frankincense and myrrh. And we even see the negative side of worship, for when the wise men came to King Herod, he wanted to know where the baby was, so he too could "worship". Of course, because Herod thought that this baby king was a threat to his throne, his worship was an intent to kill. However, Jesus' kingship was far greater than just a land or a people. In all of these examples, worship takes on different forms and different types. But they are all acts of worship.

So what about us? How do we worship? Do we worship by gathering together with other believers? Do we worship by singing? Do we worship by praying to God? Do we worship by loving others? Do we worship by helping others in need? These are just a few examples of how we can expression our reverence and adoration for God. As we worship, we wait for Jesus' return in glory. We do not know when He will return, so we continue to worship and live our lives with the hope and expectation of His return at any time. And we continue to worship.

Prayer: Dear God, we worship You for Your love and blessing, at Christmas time and throughout the year. We ask You to help us focus our hearts and minds on you in our worship. Amen.

Go, Tell it On the Mountain

While shepherds kept their watching
Over silent flocks by night,
Behold throughout the heavens,
There shone a holy light:
Go, Tell It On The Mountain,
Over the hills and everywhere;
Go, Tell It On The Mountain
That Jesus Christ is born.

The shepherds feared and trembled
When lo! above the earth
Rang out the angel chorus That
hailed our Saviour's birth: Go,
Tell It On The Mountain, Over
the hills and everywhere; Go,
Tell It On The Mountain That
Jesus Christ is born.

Down in a lowly manger Our
humble Christ was born And
God send us salvation,
That blessed Christmas morn:
Go, Tell It On The Mountain,
Over the hills and everywhere;
Go, Tell It On The Mountain
That Jesus Christ is born.

When I am a seeker,
I seek both night and day; I
seek the Lord to help me,
And He shows me the way: Go,
Tell It On The Mountain, Over
the hills and everywhere; Go,
Tell It On The Mountain That

Jesus Christ is born.

He made me a
watchman Upon the
city wall,
And if I am a
Christian, I am the
least of all.
Go, Tell It On The
Mountain, Over the hills and
everywhere; Go, Tell It On
The Mountain That Jesus
Christ is born.
Text: John Wesley Work Jr

This hymn starts with the story of the angels appearing to the shepherds, as many Christmas songs do. The reason is quite simple. Angels don't appear to people all too often! And more than that, not just one angel, but an angelic choir! The shepherds had to know, once they got past their initial shock and fear, that this was a big deal. If this were to happen in today's world, it would be something like every TV channel interrupting programming with breaking news. But this is news that is initially just for the shepherds.

The news doesn't stop with the shepherds, though. They investigate the story. They leave their sheep, head to the manger, and see the baby Jesus, just as they were told. And they quickly became the reporters of this story. More than likely, they told everyone they knew, everyone that would listen, even people who wouldn't listen, about this good news!

We are the reporters of this story as well. God has placed His faith in us, and we are called to tell the good news of the birth of Jesus to the whole world. But, there is much more to the story than that. Jesus was not only born as a baby in Bethlehem. He grew up, lived the perfect life that we cannot live, took our sin on His shoulders, and went to the cross. But still, the story doesn't end there. Jesus rose from the dead and ascended into heaven. So we have a major job ahead of us in telling the good news! Let's roll up our sleeves and get to work!

Prayer: Dear God, thank You for giving us the opportunity to share the good news, not only of the birth of Jesus, but about His life, death and resurrection with the whole world. Help us to see those opportunities and give us the words and confidence to boldly share. Amen.

Good Christian Friends, Rejoice!

Good Christian friends,
rejoice With heart and soul
and voice; Give ye heed to
what we say: Jesus Christ is
born today;
Ox and ass before him bow,
And he is in the manger
now. Christ is born today!
Christ is born today!

Good Christian friends,
rejoice With heart and soul
and voice; Now ye hear of
endless bliss: Jesus Christ
was born for this! He has
opened heaven's door, And
we are blest forever more.
Christ was born for this!
Christ was born for this!

Good Christian friends,
rejoice With heart and soul
and voice; Now ye need not
fear the grave; Jesus Christ
was born to save!
Calls you one and calls you
all To gain his everlasting
hall.
Christ was born to
save! Christ was born
to save!
Text: 14 C. Latin, translated by John Mason Neale

Rejoice! This is an expression of overwhelming and great joy. When a

www.ingramcontent.com/pod-product-compliance
Lightning Source LLC
Chambersburg PA
CBHW020939160726
47993CB00007B/2851